Easy Egg Noodle Cookbook

50 Delicious Egg Noodle Recipes

By
BookSumo Press
All rights reserved

Published by
http://www.booksumo.com

Table of Contents

German Noodles with Cabbage for Winter 5

Lunchtime Noodles 6

Hungarian Noodles 7

Homemade Egg Noodles 8

Family-Friendly Noodle Casserole 9

Sirloin Onion Egg Noodles 10

Thai Noodles 11

Hearty Chili Noodles Bake 12

Noodles & Shrimp Asian Style 13

Noodles Russian Style 14

Italian Dessert Noodles 15

Noodles Hungarian Style 16

Pennsylvanian Noodles 17

Comforting Noodle Soup 18

Buttered Parsley Noodles 19

Easy Homemade Noodles II 20

Italian Noodles with Croutons 21

Mexican Noodle Bake 22

Buttery Feta Noodles 23

A Picky Eater's Dinner 24
French Inspired Noodles 25
Wednesday's Dinner 26
Eggy-Weggy Noodle Bake 27
Chicken and Onion Egg Noodle Dump Dinner 28
Noodles Soup Tunisian Style 29
Healthy Noodles 30
Polish Noodles 31
Chinese Noodle Salad 32
Tastier Noodles Bake 33
Creamy Noodles Milanese 34
Butter Parmesan Noodles 35
Little Tike Noodles 36
Tomato Soup and Noodles 37
Japanese Style Egg Noodle 38
Authentic Amish Noodle Bake 39
Noodles Curry Thai Style 40
Fragrant Noodles 41
Country Egg Noodle Casserole 42
American Noodle Pilaf 43
Best Chinese Noodles 44

Flavorful Layered Noodle Casserole 45

Mushroom Casserole 46

Weeknight Dinner Noodles 47

Tarragon and Sage Egg Noodles 48

Perfect Buttered Noodles 49

American/French Noodle Soup 50

Simply Delicious Noodles 51

Shibuya Crossing Egg Noodles 52

Classic Yankee Noodles 53

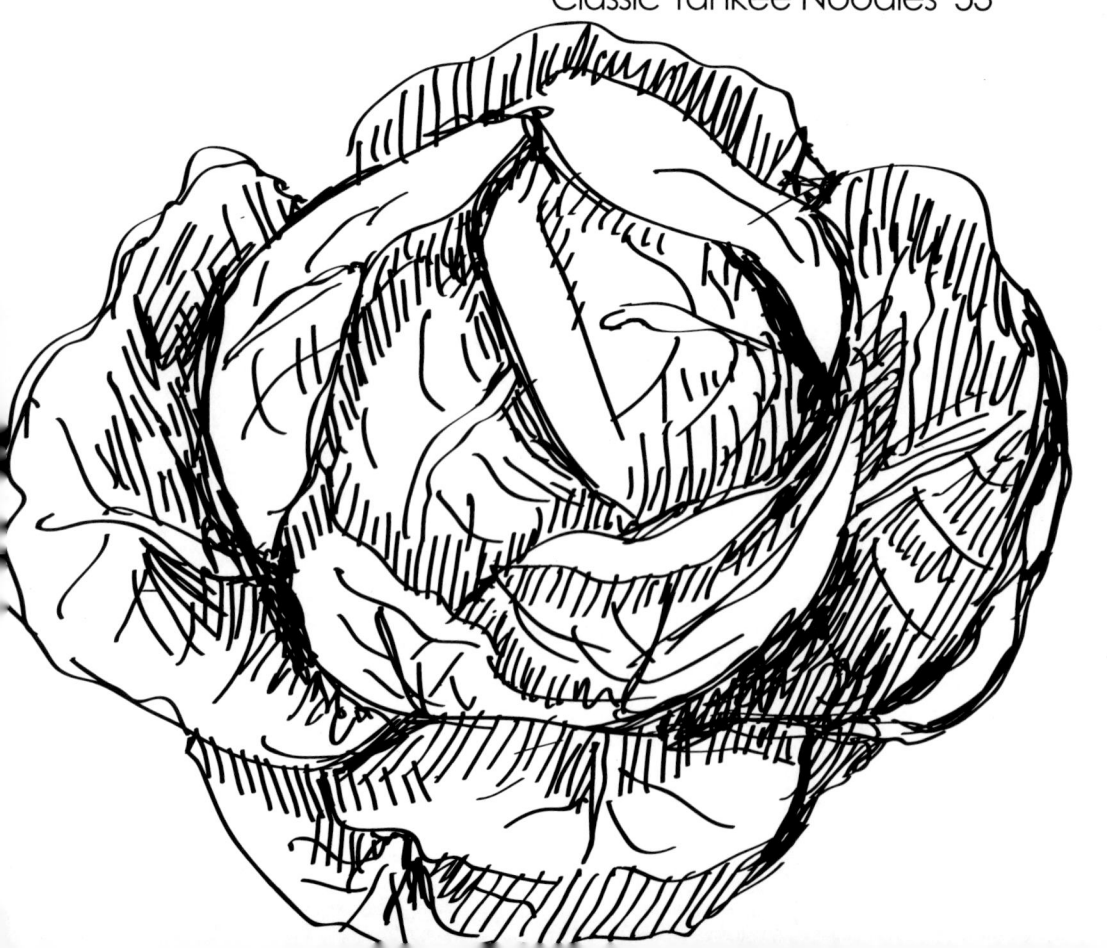

German Noodles with Cabbage for Winter

> Prep Time: 5 mins
> Total Time: 20 mins
>
> Servings per Recipe: 4
> Calories   690 kcal
> Fat   28.2 g
> Carbohydrates   93g
> Protein   19 g
> Cholesterol   155 mg
> Sodium   325 mg

Ingredients

1 (16 oz.) package egg noodles
1 stick butter
1 medium head green cabbage, chopped
salt and pepper to taste

Directions

1. In a large pan of lightly salted boiling water, cook the egg noodles for about 5 minutes.
2. Drain them well and keep everything aside.
3. Meanwhile in a large skillet, melt the butter and cook the cabbage, salt and black pepper, covered for about 5-7 minutes.
4. Stir in the cooked noodles and cook for about 5 minutes.

LUNCHTIME
Noodles

Prep Time: 10 mins
Total Time: 25 mins

Servings per Recipe: 4
Calories   335 kcal
Fat   14.1 g
Carbohydrates   43.8g
Protein   9.2 g
Cholesterol   78 mg
Sodium   117 mg

Ingredients

8 oz. wide egg noodles
1/4 C. butter
1 onion, diced
1 clove garlic, minced
4 oz. baby spinach leaves
salt and ground black pepper to taste

Directions

1. In a large pan of lightly salted boiling water, cook the egg noodles for about 8 minutes, stirring occasionally.
2. Drain them well and keep everything aside.
3. Meanwhile in a large skillet, melt the butter and on medium-high heat, sauté the onion and garlic for about 8 minutes.
4. Add the spinach, salt and black pepper and sauté for about 2 minutes.
5. Remove everything from the heat and immediately, stir in the noodles.
6. Serve immediately.

Hungarian Noodles

Prep Time: 5 mins
Total Time: 20 mins

Servings per Recipe: 8
Calories	105 kcal
Fat	3.9 g
Carbohydrates	15.1g
Protein	3 g
Cholesterol	21 mg
Sodium	157 mg

Ingredients

4 C. egg noodles
2 tbsp butter or margarine
3 C. grated kohlrabi
salt and ground black pepper to taste

Directions

1. In a large pan of lightly salted boiling water, cook the egg noodles for about 5 minutes.
2. Drain them well and keep everything aside.
3. Meanwhile in a large skillet, melt the butter and on medium heat and cook the kohlrabi, salt and pepper for about 7-10 minutes.
4. Stir in the cooked noodles and cook for about 5-7 minutes.

HOMEMADE
Egg Noodles

🥣 Prep Time: 40 mins

⏲ Total Time: 3 hr 50 mins

Servings per Recipe: 5
Calories 271 kcal
Fat 4.9 g
Carbohydrates 46.6 g
Protein 12.7 g
Cholesterol 112 mg
Sodium 294 mg

Ingredients

2 C. Durum wheat flour
1/2 tsp salt
1/4 tsp baking powder
3 eggs
water as needed

Directions

1. In a bowl, mix together the flour, baking powder and salt.
2. Add the eggs and the required amount of the water and mix till a dough forms.
3. With your hands, knead the dough till sticky.
4. Shape the dough into a ball and then cut it into quarters.
5. Place about 1/4 of the dough onto a floured surface and cut everything into 1/8-inch of thickness, then roll the dough from one end to the other.
6. Repeat with the remaining dough.
7. Cut each roll into 3/8-inch strips. (About 4-5-inch long)
8. Keep aside the noodles to dry for about 1-3 hours.
9. Cook these noodles in the boiling water till desired doneness.

Family-Friendly Noodle Casserole

Prep Time: 30 mins
Total Time: 1 hr 20 mins

Servings per Recipe: 9
Calories	524 kcal
Fat	30.9 g
Carbohydrates	42.2g
Protein	21.8 g
Cholesterol	112 mg
Sodium	723 mg

Ingredients

- 1 (12 oz.) package egg noodles
- 2 tbsp olive oil
- 2 C. fresh sliced mushrooms
- 1/2 C. chopped green bell pepper
- 1 onion, chopped
- 2 cloves garlic, minced
- 1 lb. lean ground beef
- 1 (28 oz.) can crushed tomatoes
- 1 (6 oz.) can tomato paste
- 1/4 tsp chopped fresh parsley
- 2 tsp Italian seasoning
- 1 tbsp dried oregano
- 1/4 tsp cayenne pepper
- 1 tsp salt
- ground black pepper to taste
- 1 tsp white sugar
- 1 (8 oz.) package cream cheese
- 1 (8 oz.) container sour cream
- 1/2 C. chopped green onions
- 1/2 C. grated Parmesan cheese
- 1 pinch paprika

Directions

1. In a large pan of lightly salted boiling water, cook the egg noodles till desired doneness (about 5 mins).
2. Drain them well and keep everything aside.
3. In a large skillet, heat the oil on medium heat, sauté the bell pepper, mushrooms and onion for about 5 minutes.
4. Add the beef and cook till browned completely.
5. Drain the excess fat from the skillet.
6. Stir in the tomatoes, parsley, tomato paste, Italian seasoning, oregano, cayenne pepper, salt and black pepper and simmer, covered for about 30 minutes, , stirring occasionally.
7. Set your oven to 325 degrees F and grease a large casserole dish.
8. In a bowl, mix together the sour cream, cream cheese, 1/4 C. of the Parmesan and green onion.
9. Place the cooked noodles in the bottom of the casserole dish evenly, followed by the tomato mixture, cream cheese mixture and top the mix with the remaining Parmesan and paprika.
10. Cook everything in the oven for about 45 minutes.

SIRLOIN ONION
Egg Noodles

Prep Time: 10 mins
Total Time: 6 hr 20 mins

Servings per Recipe: 8
Calories   684 kcal
Fat   16.9 g
Carbohydrates   90.6 g
Protein   38.2 g
Cholesterol   146 mg
Sodium   902 mg

Ingredients

2 lb. sirloin tips, cubed
1/2 yellow onion, chopped
2 (10.75 oz.) cans condensed cream of mushroom soup
1 C. milk
1/2 C. beef broth
1 (1.25 oz.) package beef with onion soup mix
2 (16 oz.) packages egg noodles

Directions

1. Heat a large skillet on medium-high heat and stir fry the beef and onion for about 5 minutes.
2. Meanwhile in a bowl, mix together the mushroom soup, broth, milk and soup mix.
3. Place the mixture in the skillet and bring to a simmer.
4. Reduce heat to low and simmer, covered for about 2 hours.
5. Reduce heat to its lowest setting and simmer, covered for about 4 hours.
6. In a large pan of lightly salted boiling water, cook the egg noodles for about 5 minutes.
7. Drain well.
8. Place the beef mixture over the noodles and serve.

Thai Noodles

Prep Time: 30 mins
Total Time: 1 hr 5 mins

Servings per Recipe: 6
Calories	695 kcal
Fat	32.9 g
Carbohydrates	70.5g
Protein	35.3 g
Cholesterol	187 mg
Sodium	383 mg

Ingredients

- 4 eggs
- 1 tbsp soy sauce
- 1 tbsp sesame oil
- canola oil
- 1 (12 oz.) package extra-firm tofu, cubed
- 2 C. sliced fresh mushrooms
- 2 C. broccoli florets
- 1/4 C. chopped cashews
- 1 (10 oz.) package frozen shelled edamame (green soybeans)
- 1 (16 oz.) package egg noodles
- 1/2 C. unsweetened soy milk
- 1/2 C. peanut butter
- 1/4 C. reduced-fat coconut milk
- 1 tsp tahini

Directions

1. Set your oven to 350 degrees F before doing anything else.
2. In a bowl, mix together the soy sauce and eggs.
3. Heat a nonstick skillet on medium heat and cook the egg mixture for about 3-5 minutes.
4. Transfer the cooked eggs onto a cutting board and chop them.
5. In a large skillet, heat both the oils on medium heat and cook the tofu for about 8-10 minutes.
6. Transfer the tofu into a bowl.
7. In the same skillet, add the broccoli and mushrooms and cook for about 5-7 minutes.
8. In a baking dish, place the cashews and cook them in the oven for about 8-12 minutes.
9. In a microwave safe bowl, place the edamame and microwave it, covered for about 1-2 minutes.
10. In a large pan of lightly salted boiling water, cook the egg noodles for about 8 minutes.
11. Drain them well and keep everything aside.
12. In a large pan, mix together the remaining ingredients on medium heat and cook, stirring continuously, for about 2-4 minutes.
13. Add the noodles, tofu, chopped eggs, edamame and broccoli mixture and toss to combine.
14. Serve with a topping of roasted cashews.

HEARTY CHILI
Noodles Bake

🥣 Prep Time: 15 mins
🕐 Total Time: 50 mins

Servings per Recipe: 6
Calories   510 kcal
Fat   20 g
Carbohydrates   49 g
Protein   27.6 g
Cholesterol   111 mg
Sodium   1129 mg

Ingredients

1 (12 oz.) package wide egg noodles
1 lb. ground beef
1 onion, chopped
3 cloves garlic, minced
2 (15 oz.) cans tomato sauce
1 (8 oz.) can tomato sauce
15 fluid oz. water
1 C. broth
1 tbsp ground cumin
1 tsp dried oregano
1/2 tsp cayenne pepper
1 C. shredded sharp Cheddar cheese

Directions

1. Set your oven to 350 degrees F before doing anything else and grease a 14x9-inch baking dish.
2. In a large pan of lightly salted boiling water, cook the egg noodles for about 5 minutes, stirring occasionally.
3. Drain them well and keep everything aside.
4. Heat a large skillet on medium-high heat and cook the beef till browned completely.
5. Add the onion and garlic and stir fry them till the onion becomes tender.
6. Add the tomato sauce, broth, water, oregano, cumin and cayenne pepper and bring to a simmer.
7. Stir in the pasta and place the mixture into the prepared baking dish.
8. Top everything with the cheddar cheese and cook everything in the oven for about 20 minutes.

Noodles
& Shrimp Asian Style

🥣 Prep Time: 20 mins
🕐 Total Time: 30 mins

Servings per Recipe: 6
Calories   322 kcal
Fat   6.3 g
Carbohydrates   49 g
Protein   15.1 g
Cholesterol   83 mg
Sodium   616 mg

Ingredients

1 lb. fresh Chinese egg noodles
2 tbsp olive oil
1/3 C. chopped onion
1 clove garlic, chopped
3/4 C. broccoli florets
1/2 C. chopped red bell pepper
2 C. cooked shrimp
1/2 C. sliced water chestnuts, drained

1/2 C. baby corn, drained
1/2 C. canned sliced bamboo shoots, drained
3 tbsp oyster sauce
1 tbsp red pepper flakes, or to taste

Directions

1. In a large pan of lightly salted boiling water, cook the egg noodles for about 1-2 minutes.
2. Drain them well and keep everything aside.
3. In a large skillet, heat the oil on medium-high heat, sauté the onion and garlic for about 1 minute.
4. Stir in the bell pepper and broccoli and stir fry everything for about 3 minutes.
5. Stir in the remaining ingredients and cook for about 3 more minutes.
6. Serve the noodles with a topping of the veggie mixture.

NOODLES
Russian Style

Prep Time: 10 mins
Total Time: 20 mins

Servings per Recipe: 6
Calories   363 kcal
Fat   24.2 g
Carbohydrates   27.1g
Protein   9.9 g
Cholesterol   78 mg
Sodium   394 mg

Ingredients

1 (8 oz.) package egg noodles
2 C. sour cream
1/2 C. grated Parmesan cheese, divided
1 tbsp chopped fresh chives
1/2 tsp salt
1/8 tsp ground black pepper
2 tbsp butter

Directions

1. In a large pan of lightly salted boiling water, cook the egg noodles for about 8-10 minutes.
2. Drain well.
3. Add the butter and stir to combine.
4. Meanwhile in a bowl, mix together 1/4 C. of the cheese, sour cream, chives, salt and black pepper.
5. Place the mixture over the noodles and gently, stir to combine.
6. Serve immediately with a topping of the remaining cheese.

Italian Dessert Noodles

🥣 Prep Time: 20 mins
🕐 Total Time: 1 hr 10 mins

Servings per Recipe: 15
Calories	243 kcal
Fat	12.6 g
Carbohydrates	29.1g
Protein	4.9 g
Cholesterol	82 mg
Sodium	221 mg

Ingredients

1 (12 oz.) package wide egg noodles
1/2 C. butter, melted
3/4 C. white sugar
3/4 C. raisins
3/4 C. coarsely chopped pecans
1 tsp salt
4 eggs, beaten
1/4 tsp ground cinnamon

Directions

1. Set your oven to 375 degrees F before doing anything else and grease a 12x8-inch baking dish with some melted butter evenly.
2. In a large pan of lightly salted boiling water, cook the egg noodles for about 8-10 minutes.
3. Drain well.
4. In a large bowl, mix together the remaining butter, noodles, eggs, pecans, raisins, sugar and salt.
5. Transfer the mixture into the prepared baking dish and sprinkle with the cinnamon.
6. Cook everything in the oven for about 55 minutes.

NOODLES
Hungarian Style

Prep Time: 15 mins
Total Time: 50 mins

Servings per Recipe: 6
Calories 414 kcal
Fat 22.6 g
Carbohydrates 35.1g
Protein 18.1 g
Cholesterol 77 mg
Sodium 809 mg

Ingredients

- 1 (8 oz.) package fine egg noodles
- 2 C. cottage cheese
- 2 C. sour cream
- 1/2 C. chopped onions
- 2 tbsp Worcestershire sauce
- 2 tbsp poppy seeds
- 1 tsp salt
- 1 tbsp grated Parmesan cheese
- 1 pinch ground paprika

Directions

1. Set your oven to 350 degrees F before doing anything else and grease a large casserole dish.
2. In a large pan of lightly salted boiling water, cook the egg noodles for about 5 minutes, stirring occasionally.
3. Drain them well and keep everything aside.
4. In a large bowl, add the noodles and remaining ingredients except the Parmesan cheese and paprika and mix well.
5. Transfer the mixture into the prepared casserole dish evenly and top with the Parmesan cheese and paprika.
6. Cook everything in the oven for about 30 minutes.

Pennsylvanian Noodles

- Prep Time: 5 mins
- Total Time: 15 mins

Servings per Recipe: 4
Calories   320.6
Fat   14.0g
Cholesterol   78.3mg
Sodium   113.2mg
Carbohydrates   40.6g
Protein   8.1g

Ingredients

8 oz. wide egg noodles
1/4-1/2 C. salted butter

Directions

1. In large pan of boiling water, prepare the egg noodles according to the package's directions.
2. Drain well and transfer into a large bowl.
3. Meanwhile in a small frying pan, add the butter and melt, stirring till the butter starts to become brown.
4. Pour melted butter, salt and black pepper and stir to coat well.

COMFORTING
Noodle Soup

Prep Time: 10 mins
Total Time: 36 mins

Servings per Recipe: 4
Calories 536.3
Fat 12.8g
Cholesterol 115.7mg
Sodium 629.1mg
Carbohydrates 55.8g
Protein 51.1g

Ingredients

2 tsp olive oil or 2 tsp vegetable oil
2 leeks, cleaned and chopped
2 carrots, peeled and chopped
1 garlic clove, minced
1 stalk celery, chopped
3 - 4 C. cooked turkey, shredded
2 - 3 bay leaves
2 tsp dried thyme
1/2 tsp salt
1/4 tsp fresh ground black pepper
8 C. reduced-chicken broth
6 oz. egg noodles, uncooked
1 C. frozen green pea
2 tbsp fresh parsley leaves, chopped

Directions

1. In a large pan, heat the oil on medium heat, sauté the carrots, celery, leeks and garlic for about 4 minutes.
2. Stir in the turkey, thyme, bay leaves and black pepper.
3. Add the broth and bring to a boil.
4. Reduce the heat to medium-low and simmer, covered partially for about 10 minutes.
5. Uncover and again bring to a boil, then stir in the noodles.
6. Simmer for about 10 minutes.
7. Stir in the peas and simmer for about 1 minute.
8. Remove everything from the heat and discard the bay leaves.
9. Stir in the parsley and serve.

Buttered Parsley Noodles

Prep Time: 10 mins
Total Time: 15 mins

Servings per Recipe: 6
Calories   287.4
Fat   10.2g
Cholesterol   68.2mg
Sodium   14.0mg
Carbohydrates   40.7g
Protein   8.2g

Ingredients

kosher salt
1 (12 oz.) packages wide egg noodles
4 - 6 tbsp cold unsalted butter, cut into bits
3 tbsp flat leaf parsley, chopped
fresh ground black pepper

Directions

1. In a large pan of lightly salted boiling water, cook the egg noodles for about 5 minutes, stirring occasionally.
2. Drain well, reserving 1/4 C. of the cooking liquid.
3. In a medium skillet, add the reserved hot cooking liquid on low heat.
4. Slowly, add the butter, beating continuously till a creamy sauce forms.
5. Stir in the parsley, salt and black pepper.
6. Add the noodles and toss to coat well.
7. Serve immediately.

EASY HOMEMADE
Noodles II

Prep Time: 5 mins
Total Time: 25 mins

Servings per Recipe: 1
Calories   114.3
Fat   5.7g
Cholesterol   223.2mg
Sodium   90.3mg
Carbohydrates   7.0g
Protein   8.0g

Ingredients

6 eggs, beaten
1/2 C. water, room temperature
1/4 C. potato starch
salt
oil, for pan

Directions

1. In a bowl, mix together the potato starch and water.
2. Slowly, add the beaten eggs and salt, beating continuously till well combined.
3. Heat a lightly greased skillet on medium heat and add a thin layer of the egg mixture and cook till set.
4. Flip the side and immediately transfer onto a plate, uncooked side up.
5. Tightly roll it and cut everything into 1/4-inch circles.
6. Repeat with the remaining egg mixture.
7. These noodles can be used in any soup.

Italian Noodles with Croutons

Prep Time: 5 mins
Total Time: 17 mins

Servings per Recipe: 4
Calories	565.3
Fat	27.2g
Cholesterol	132.8mg
Sodium	145.0mg
Carbohydrates	67.3g
Protein	13.3g

Ingredients

- 12 oz. egg noodles
- 1/2 C. unsalted butter
- 2 slices white bread (day old is good), torn
- 1 pinch salt
- 1/4 tsp pepper

Directions

1. In large pan of boiling water, prepare the egg noodles according to the package's directions.
2. Meanwhile for croutons in a small frying pan, melt the butter on medium heat and cook the bread pieces till lightly crispy.
3. Stir in the salt and black pepper and remove everything from the heat.
4. In serving bowl, mix together the noodles and croutons and serve.

MEXICAN
Noodle Bake

Prep Time: 20 mins
Total Time: 1 hr 20 mins

Servings per Recipe: 4
Calories 708.1
Fat 37.2g
Cholesterol 188.0mg
Sodium 797.9mg
Carbohydrates 47.6g
Protein 44.5g

Ingredients

1 (8 oz.) packages wide egg noodles
1 lb lean ground beef
6 green onions, sliced
2 large garlic cloves, minced
3/4 tsp salt, divided
1 (26 oz.) jars tomato and basil pasta sauce
1/8 tsp pepper
1 (8 oz.) packages ricotta cheese
1 C. sour cream
1/2 C. shredded parmesan cheese

Directions

1. Set your oven to 350 degrees F before doing anything else and lightly grease a large baking dish.
2. Heat a large skillet on medium-high heat and cook the beef with green onions, garlic and 1/2 tsp of the salt till the beef is browned completely.
3. Drain the excess grease from the skillet.
4. Stir in the pasta sauce and black pepper and reduce the heat.
5. Simmer, covered for about 20 minutes.
6. Meanwhile cook the noodles according to the package's directions.
7. Drain well and transfer into a large bowl with 1 C. of the sour cream, ricotta and remaining salt, then mix well.
8. Place half of the noodle mixture in the bottom of the prepared baking dish, followed by half of the beef mixture.
9. Repeat the layers and cook everything in the oven for about 25 minutes.
10. Sprinkle with Parmesan and cook everything in the oven for about 5 minutes more.

Buttery Feta Noodles

Prep Time: 10 mins
Total Time: 30 mins

Servings per Recipe: 6
Calories   506.8
Fat   25.1g
Cholesterol   131.2mg
Sodium   460.2mg
Carbohydrates   55.4g
Protein   15.1g

Ingredients

1 lb dried egg noodles
1/2 C. butter
6 oz. greek feta, crumbled

Directions

1. Prepare the egg noodles according to the package's directions (boil for 5 mins).
2. In a small pan, melt the butter on low heat for about 6 minutes and then remove everything from the heat.
3. On a large platter, place about 1/3 of the noodles and top them with 1/3 of the feta cheese
4. Repeat the layers twice and top everything with the butter, salt and black pepper and toss to coat.

A PICKY EATER'S
Dinner

🥣 Prep Time: 10 mins
⏱ Total Time: 25 mins

Servings per Recipe: 6
Calories   522.5
Fat   17.0g
Cholesterol   79.8mg
Sodium   648.3mg
Carbohydrates   62.8g
Protein   32.8g

Ingredients

1 lb lean ground beef
8 oz. Velveeta cheese, cubed
1/4 C. low-fat milk
1 tbsp chopped garlic
1 tbsp Worcestershire sauce
1 tbsp onion powder
salt and pepper

1 lb egg noodles

Directions

1. In large pan of boiling water, prepare the egg noodles according to the package's directions, then drain well.
2. Meanwhile heat a large skillet on medium heat and cook the beef till browned completely.
3. Stir in the onion powder, salt and black pepper.
4. Meanwhile in another small pan, add the Velveeta cheese cubes on medium-low heat.
5. Stir in the milk, Worcestershire sauce, garlic, onion powder, salt and pepper and cook, stirring continuously till smooth.
6. In the pan of beef, add the Velveeta sauce and noodles and stir to combine.
7. Serve immediately.

French Inspired Noodles

Prep Time: 30 mins
Total Time: 2 hr 30 mins

Servings per Recipe: 9
Calories   613.0
Fat   31.2g
Cholesterol   143.3mg
Sodium   985.3mg
Carbohydrates   36.2g
Protein   38.9g

Ingredients

1/3 C. all-purpose flour
2 tsp salt, divided
3/4 tsp black pepper, divided
2 1/4 lb. beef stew meat
3 turkey bacon, slices chopped and divided
1 C. onion, chopped
1 C. carrot, sliced
4 garlic cloves, minced
1 1/2 C. fish stock
1 (14 oz.) cans beef broth
8 C. mushrooms, halved
2 tbsp tomato paste
2 tsp thyme
2 bay leaves
1 (16 oz.) packages frozen pearl onions
7 C. egg noodles, cooked
3 tbsp parsley

Directions

1. In a zip-top plastic bag, add the beef, flour, 1 tsp of the salt and 1/4 tsp of the black pepper and seal the bag, then shake to coat completely.
2. Heat a large Dutch oven on medium-high heat cook half of the bacon till browned completely.
3. Transfer the bacon onto a paper towel lined plate to drain.
4. In the same skillet, add the beef and cook for about 5 minutes.
5. Transfer the beef onto a plate and cover everything with some foil to keep warm.
6. Repeat with the remaining bacon and beef.
7. In the same pan, add the carrot, onion and garlic and sauté for about 5 minutes.
8. Stir in the broth and stock and with the spoon scrape the pan to loosen any browned bits.
9. Add the beef, bacon, salt, black pepper and remaining ingredients except the noodles and parsley and bring to a boil.
10. Reduce the heat and simmer, covered for about 45 minutes.
11. Uncover and simmer for about 1 hour.
12. Remove everything from the heat and discard the bay leaves.
13. Place the beef mixture over the noodles and serve with a topping of the parsley.

WEDNESDAY'S
Dinner

Prep Time: 15 mins
Total Time: 45 mins

Servings per Recipe: 4
Calories 904.4
Fat 23.9g
Cholesterol 233.9mg
Sodium 1740.2mg
Carbohydrates 96.2g
Protein 74.5g

Ingredients

2 lb. any type boneless skinless chicken
1 (12 oz.) packages egg noodles
2 (10 3/4 oz.) cans cream of chicken soup
1/2 C. milk
1 (10 oz.) packages frozen green peas
1 - 2 tbsp olive oil
8 oz. canned mushrooms

1 small onion, finely chopped
1 tsp minced garlic
1 tsp fresh ground black pepper

Directions

1. In a pan, heat about 1 tbsp of the oil and cook the chicken till done completely.
2. Transfer the chicken into a bowl, then cut it into bite sized pieces.
3. In the same pan, heat the remaining oil on medium-high heat, sauté the onion, mushrooms and garlic till tender.
4. Drain the excess grease from the pan.
5. Stir in the chicken, milk, chicken soup, peas and black pepper and simmer everything for about 15 minutes.
6. Meanwhile, prepare the egg noodles according to the package's directions.
7. Drain well.
8. Add the noodles to the pan with the chicken mixture and gently, stir to combine.
9. Serve the dinner with some biscuits or rolls.

Eggy-Weggy Noodle Bake

Prep Time: 15 mins
Total Time: 1 hr 25 mins

Servings per Recipe: 9
Calories	336 kcal
Fat	16.5 g
Carbohydrates	26.2g
Protein	20.9 g
Cholesterol	84 mg
Sodium	744 mg

Ingredients

- 1 tbsp olive oil
- 1 lb. extra lean ground beef
- 1/2 tsp ground dried thyme
- 1 (1.5 oz.) envelope spaghetti sauce seasoning mix
- 1 (6 oz.) can tomato paste
- 3 C. water
- salt and black pepper to taste
- 1 (8 oz.) package egg noodles
- 1 (3 oz.) package cream cheese, softened
- 1 tbsp chopped fresh parsley
- 1/4 C. grated Parmesan cheese
- 1 (8 oz.) container sour cream
- 1 C. shredded mozzarella cheese, divided

Directions

1. In a large skillet, heat the oil on medium-high heat and stir fry the beef for about 5-7 minutes.
2. Drain the excess grease from the skillet.
3. Stir in the tomato paste, spaghetti sauce seasoning mix, thyme, salt, black pepper and water and bring to a boil.
4. Reduce heat to medium-low and simmer, covered for about 25 minutes, stirring occasionally.
5. Set your oven to 350 degrees F and grease a 13x9-inch baking dish.
6. Meanwhile in a large pan of lightly salted boiling water, cook the egg noodles for about 5 minutes.
7. Drain them well and keep everything aside.
8. In a bowl, add the cream cheese, Parmesan and parsley and mix till smooth.
9. Stir in the 3/4 of the shredded mozzarella cheese and sour cream.
10. In the bottom of the prepared baking dish, place half of the noodles, followed by the half of the beef mixture and half of the cream cheese mixture.
11. Repeat the layers once and top with the remaining mozzarella cheese.
12. Cook everything in the oven for about 35 minutes.

CHICKEN AND ONION
Egg Noodle Dump Dinner

Prep Time: 30 mins
Total Time: 8 h 30 mins

Servings per Recipe: 6
Calories   311 kcal
Fat   3.5 g
Carbohydrates   42g
Protein   26.4 g
Cholesterol   93 mg
Sodium   81 mg

Ingredients

4 skinless, boneless chicken breast halves
6 C. water
1 onion, chopped
2 stalks celery, chopped
salt and pepper to taste
1 (12 oz.) package egg noodles

Directions

1. In a slow cooker, add all the ingredients except the noodles.
2. Set the slow cooker on Low and cook, covered for about 6-8 hours.
3. Remove the chicken from the slow cooker and chop into bite-sized pieces.
4. Now, set the slow cooker on High.
5. Stir in the noodles and cook till the noodles are cooked through.
6. Stir in the chicken and serve.

Noodles Soup Tunisian Style

Prep Time: 15 mins
Total Time: 50 mins

Servings per Recipe: 4
Calories   578.8
Fat   19.1g
Cholesterol   38.3mg
Sodium   1402.6mg
Carbohydrates   77.8g
Protein   578.8

Ingredients

- 1 tsp cumin seed
- 1 lb. swiss chard, stems and center ribs chopped and leaves coarsely chopped (reserve separately)
- 1 medium red onion, chopped
- 2 large garlic cloves, minced
- 3 tbsp extra-virgin olive oil
- 2 tbsp tomato paste
- 2 quarts rich and flavorful chicken broth
- 1 - 2 tbsp harissa
- 1 tbsp fresh lemon juice
- 1 (19 oz.) can chickpeas, drained & rinsed
- 4 oz. fine egg noodles
- 4 lemon wedges, for accompaniment

Directions

1. In a nonstick skillet, toast the cumin seeds on medium heat, stirring continuously.
2. Remove everything from the heat and let it cool completely.
3. In a grinder, grind the cumin seeds till powdered.
4. In a large heavy pot, heat the oil on medium heat and stir fry the chard stems, onion, garlic 1/2 tsp of cumin, salt and black pepper for about 10 minutes.
5. Stir in the tomato paste and stir fry for about 2 minutes.
6. Stir in the broth, lemon juice and harissa and simmer, covered for about 15 minutes.
7. Stir in the chard leaves, noodles, chickpeas and a little salt and simmer, covered for about 5 minutes.
8. Serve hot with a sprinkling of the remaining cumin.

HEALTHY
Noodles

Prep Time: 5 mins
Total Time: 20 mins

Servings per Recipe: 4
Calories 298.3
Fat 17.3g
Cholesterol 77.1mg
Sodium 303.5mg
Carbohydrates 10.8g
Protein 24.1g

Ingredients

1 lb ground beef
2 onions, chopped
2 (4 oz.) cans mushrooms
1/4 tsp garlic powder
pepper
salt
1 C. beef broth

2 tbsp cornstarch
parmesan cheese
egg noodles

Directions

1. In a large pan of lightly salted boiling water, cook the egg noodles for about 10-12 minutes.
2. Drain them well and keep everything aside.
3. Heat a large skillet and cook the beef with mushrooms and onions till browned completely.
4. Stir in the broth, garlic, salt and black pepper and simmer for about 10 minutes.
5. Stir in the cornstarch.
6. Place the beef mixture over the noodles and serve with a topping of cheese.

Polish Noodles

Prep Time: 5 mins
Total Time: 25 mins

Servings per Recipe: 4
Calories　　　　563.9
Fat　　　　　　16.6g
Cholesterol　　126.2mg
Sodium　　　　138.5mg
Carbohydrates　86.9g
Protein　　　　17.3g

Ingredients

4 C. cabbage (sliced)
1 small onion (chopped)
1/4 C. butter
1 lb wide egg noodles
salt and pepper
sour cream

Directions

1. In large pan of boiling water, prepare the egg noodles according to the package's directions.
2. Drain well.
3. Meanwhile in a large skillet, melt the butter and sauté the onion till tender.
4. Stir in the cabbage and sauté for about 5 minutes.
5. Add the noodles, sour cream, salt and black pepper and mix well.

CHINESE
Noodle Salad

🥣 Prep Time: 10 mins
🕐 Total Time: 20 mins

Servings per Recipe: 4
Calories   322.9
Fat   10.9g
Cholesterol   43.2mg
Sodium   505.0mg
Carbohydrates   46.7g
Protein   11.5g

Ingredients

4 C. egg noodles, cooked
1 large avocado, cubed
1 C. imitation crabmeat, diced
1/2 C. water chestnut, chopped (canned)
1 red bell pepper, diced
1 tbsp horseradish cream
1/2 C. low-fat mayonnaise

1 tbsp fresh parsley, finely chopped
1 tbsp fresh chives, finely chopped
salt and pepper, to taste

Directions

1. In a large bowl, mix together the noodles, crabmeat, avocado, bell pepper and water chestnuts.
2. In another bowl, add the remaining ingredients and beat till well combined.
3. Pour the dressing over the salad and toss to coat well.

Tastier Noodles Bake

Prep Time: 20 mins
Total Time: 50 mins

Servings per Recipe: 4
Calories   740.5
Fat   49.5g
Cholesterol   195.3mg
Sodium   772.2mg
Carbohydrates   24.8g
Protein   47.5g

Ingredients

1 lb ground beef
1/2 C. green pepper
1/2 C. onion
1 tsp seasoning salt
1/8 tsp pepper
8 oz. tomato sauce with basic and garlic
4 -6 oz. egg noodles
1 C. cottage cheese
1 C. sour cream
1 1/2 C. shredded sharp cheddar cheese, divided
1/2 C. grated parmesan cheese

Directions

1. Set your oven to 350 degrees F before doing anything else and grease a casserole dish.
2. Heat a large skillet and cook the beef with the green pepper and onion till browned completely.
3. Stir in the tomato sauce and seasoning and simmer for about 5 minutes.
4. Meanwhile prepare the egg noodles according to the package's directions.
5. Drain well.
6. In a bowl, mix together the noodles, sour cream, cottage cheese and 1/2 C. of the cheddar cheese.
7. In the bottom of the prepared casserole dish, place half of the noodles mixture, followed by the beef mixture and the remaining noodle mixture.
8. Top everything with the remaining cheddar cheese and cook everything in the oven for about 20 minutes.
9. Sprinkle the dish with the Parmesan and cook everything in the oven for about 10 minutes.

CREAMY NOODLES
Milanese

🥣 Prep Time: 5 mins
🕐 Total Time: 20 mins

Servings per Recipe: 4
Calories   386.8
Fat   19.3g
Cholesterol   95.0mg
Sodium   201.6mg
Carbohydrates   42.1g
Protein   11.4g

Ingredients

8 oz. wide egg noodles
1/4 C. butter or 1/4 C. margarine, softened
1/2 C. half-and-half
1/4 C. grated parmesan cheese
2 1/4 tsp Italian salad dressing mix

Directions

1. In large pan of boiling water, prepare the egg noodles till they reach the desired doneness.
2. Drain well.
3. In a pan of pasta, add the butter and noodles and toss to coat.
4. Add the remaining ingredients and mix till well combined.
5. Serve immediately.

Butter Parmesan Noodles

Prep Time: 10 mins
Total Time: 10 mins

Servings per Recipe: 1
Calories   320.6
Fat   14.0g
Cholesterol   78.4mg
Sodium   113.3mg
Carbohydrates   40.6g
Protein   8.1g

Ingredients

1 1/2 C. egg noodles
salt
1 tbsp butter, chopped
flat leaf parsley
fresh ground black pepper
1/4 C. freshly grated parmigiano-reggiano cheese

Directions

1. In a large pan of lightly salted boiling water, cook the egg noodles for about 5 minutes.
2. Drain well and transfer into a bowl.
3. Add the butter and cheese and toss to coat well.
4. Serve with a sprinkling of the parsley and black pepper.

LITTLE TIKE
Noodles

🥣 Prep Time: 5 mins
🕐 Total Time: 20 mins

Servings per Recipe: 6
Calories 157.5
Fat 10.2g
Cholesterol 38.1mg
Sodium 185.0mg
Carbohydrates 11.3g
Protein 5.3g

Ingredients

9 oz. medium egg noodles, uncooked
3 tbsp butter
1/4 tsp seasoning salt
3 tbsp sour cream
1/2 C. freshly grated parmesan cheese

Directions

1. In a large pan of lightly salted boiling water, cook the egg noodles till desired doneness.
2. Drain well and return in the pan.
3. Add the butter and stir to coat well.
4. Stir in the remaining ingredients and serve.

Tomato Soup and Noodles

Prep Time: 10 mins
Total Time: 30 mins

Servings per Recipe: 8
Calories   303.9
Fat   7.2g
Cholesterol   75.3mg
Sodium   251.2mg
Carbohydrates   39.6g
Protein   20.3g

Ingredients

6 C. broad egg noodles, uncooked
1 lb extra lean ground beef
1 C. onion, sliced
1/2 C. green pepper, chopped
1 (10 oz.) cans mushrooms, undrained
1 (10 oz.) cans condensed tomato soup
1/2 C. light cream cheese spread

1 tbsp Worcestershire sauce
fresh parsley, chopped

Directions

1. In large pan of boiling water, prepare the egg noodles according to the package's directions.
2. Drain well.
3. Heat a large skillet on medium heat and cook the beef till browned completely.
4. Drain the excess grease from the skillet.
5. Stir in the peppers and onions and cook till tender.
6. Stir in the remaining ingredients and cook for about 5 minutes.
7. Place the beef mixture over the noodles and serve with a garnishing of the parsley.

JAPANESE STYLE
Egg Noodle

🥣 Prep Time: 10 mins
🕐 Total Time: 25 mins

Servings per Recipe: 6
Calories 152.2
Fat 5.4g
Cholesterol 15.9mg
Sodium 896.9mg
Carbohydrates 22.6g
Protein 4.3g

Ingredients

1/4 lb fine dried egg noodles
1 medium red onion, sliced thinly
1 1/2 C. fresh shiitake mushrooms, sliced thinly
1 tbsp vegetable oil
3 tbsp soy sauce
1 tbsp balsamic vinegar
2 tsp brown sugar
1 tsp salt
1 tbsp sesame oil
fresh parsley leaves, to garnish

Directions

1. In a large pan of lightly salted boiling water, cook the egg noodles for about 5 minutes.
2. Drain them well and keep everything aside.
3. In a large skillet, heat the oil and sauté the mushrooms and onion for about 3 minutes.
4. Stir in the noodles, brown sugar, vinegar, soy sauce and salt and toss to coat well.
5. Stir in the sesame oil and serve with a garnishing of parsley.

Authentic Amish Noodle Bake

🥣 Prep Time: 30 mins
🕒 Total Time: 1 hr 15 mins

Servings per Recipe: 4
Calories   601.5
Fat   26.7g
Cholesterol   147.0mg
Sodium   261.8mg
Carbohydrates   57.3g
Protein   32.2g

Ingredients

1/2 C. onion, finely chopped
1 C. celery, finely chopped
3 tbsp butter
3 tbsp flour
1 tbsp mustard
1 1/2 C. milk
2 C. cooked turkey (chopped fine)
1 C. frozen green pea, thawed
8 oz. egg noodles, cooked and drained
salt and pepper, to taste
breadcrumbs
butter

Directions

1. Set your oven to 350 degrees F before doing anything else and grease a casserole dish.
2. In a large skillet, melt 3 tbsp of the butter and sauté the celery and onion till tender.
3. Add the mustard and flour and cook, stirring continuously for about 2 minutes.
4. Slowly, add the milk, stirring continuously, and cook until thickened.
5. Add the peas and turkey and stir to combine.
6. Add the noodles, salt and black pepper and toss to coat well.
7. Transfer the mixture into the prepared casserole dish and sprinkle everything with the bread crumbs.
8. Top the dish with the remaining butter in dots and cook everything in the oven for about 45 minutes.

NOODLES CURRY
Thai Style

🥣 Prep Time: 10 mins
🕐 Total Time: 25 mins

Servings per Recipe: 4
Calories   217.4
Fat   14.3g
Cholesterol   46.8mg
Sodium   477.3mg
Carbohydrates   7.9g
Protein   14.0g

Ingredients

350 g fresh egg noodles, flat
250 g ground beef
2 C. snow peas, sliced
1 tbsp minced garlic clove
1 tbsp red curry paste
1 C. low-fat coconut milk
1 C. chicken stock

1 tbsp curry powder
1 pinch turmeric powder
1 tbsp fish sauce
1 tbsp lime juice

Directions

1. Prepare the egg noodles according to the package's directions.
2. Drain well and transfer into a bowl, then cover to keep warm.
3. In a pan, add the coconut milk on low heat.
4. Cook till heated through, then stir in the curry paste.
5. Add the remaining ingredients except the snow peas and beef and stir fry for about 2 minutes.
6. Stir in the beef and cook till the beef is done completely.
7. Stir in the cooked noodles and snow peas and serve immediately.

Fragrant Noodles

🥣 Prep Time: 10 mins
🕐 Total Time: 25 mins

Servings per Recipe: 6
Calories   139.0
Fat   4.4g
Cholesterol   31.5mg
Sodium   6.5mg
Carbohydrates   20.5g
Protein   4.2g

Ingredients

6 oz. wide egg noodles
1 1/2 tsp poppy seeds
1 1/2 tbsp unsalted butter
1/2 tsp finely grated fresh lemon zest
2 tbsp fresh chives

Directions

1. Prepare the egg noodles according to the package's directions.
2. Drain well, reserving about 1/2 C. of the cooking liquid.
3. Meanwhile heat a small skillet on medium-low heat and toast the poppy seeds for about 2 minutes, stirring continuously.
4. Heat a pan and add in the butter and lemon zest and tilt the pan to coat.
5. Add noodles and enough of the reserved cooking liquid and toss to coat.
6. Stir in the poppy seeds, chives, salt and pepper and serve.

COUNTRY Egg Noodle Casserole

🥣 Prep Time: 10 mins
🕐 Total Time: 55 mins

Servings per Recipe: 6
Calories 538.6
Fat 33.6g
Cholesterol 80.8mg
Sodium 1702.9mg
Carbohydrates 33.8g
Protein 24.5g

Ingredients

3 C. egg noodles, uncooked
1 tbsp oil
1 tbsp butter
1 lb cooked ground Italian chicken sausage
1/4 C. mushroom, chopped
1/2 yellow onion, chopped
2 tbsp garlic, minced

1 (26 oz.) jars spaghetti sauce
1 C. mozzarella cheese, shredded, divided
5 -10 slices beef pepperoni

Directions

1. Set your oven to 350 degrees F before doing anything else.
2. In large pan of boiling water, prepare the egg noodles according to the package's directions.
3. Drain well.
4. Meanwhile in a large skillet, melt the butter and onion and sauté the onion, mushrooms and garlic till cooked through.
5. Stir in the cooked sausage and sauté for about 5-7 minutes.
6. In the bottom of a large casserole dish, spread about 2 tbsp of the spaghetti sauce.
7. Place about 1/2 of the cooked noodles, sausage mixture, 1/2 of the remaining spaghetti sauce and 1/2 C. of the mozzarella cheese.
8. Now, place the remaining noodles, remaining sauce and remaining cheese and top with the pepperoni slices.
9. Cook everything in the oven for about 40-45 minutes.

American Noodle Pilaf

Prep Time: 5 mins
Total Time: 35 mins

Servings per Recipe: 4
Calories 292.7
Fat 12.1g
Cholesterol 34.4mg
Sodium 423.5mg
Carbohydrates 40.6g
Protein 4.5g

Ingredients

1/4 C. butter
1 C. long grain rice
1/2 C. uncooked fine egg noodles
2 3/4 C. fat free chicken broth
2 tbsp minced fresh parsley

Directions

1. In a pan, melt the butter and cook the noodles and rice, stirring continuously for about 3 minutes.
2. Add the broth and bring to a boil.
3. Reduce the heat and simmer, covered for about 20-25 minutes.
4. Stir in the parsley and serve.

BEST CHINESE
Noodles

🥣 Prep Time: 10 mins
🕐 Total Time: 35 mins

Servings per Recipe: 2
Calories   776.2
Fat   32.3g
Cholesterol   367.7mg
Sodium   632.9mg
Carbohydrates   83.8g
Protein   35.6g

Ingredients

8 oz. Chinese egg noodles
6 links beef sausages
2 eggs, hard boiled
4 green onions
soy sauce
sesame seeds

Directions

1. In a pan of boiling water, cook the sausage links for about 20-25 minutes.
2. Drain them well and keep everything aside to cool.
3. Remove the casing and cut each sausage into 1/2-inch pieces.
4. Peel the boiled eggs and then grate into a bowl.
5. Prepare the egg noodles according to the package's directions (boil for 5 mins).
6. Drain well.
7. Place the noodles in a serving bowl and top with the sausage, grated eggs, green onions, soy sauce and sesame seeds

Flavorful Layered Noodle Casserole

Prep Time:	20 mins
Total Time:	50 mins

Servings per Recipe: 4
Calories   1135.4
Fat   79.9g
Cholesterol   227.3mg
Sodium   1076.5mg
Carbohydrates   68.5g
Protein   35.5g

Ingredients

- 15 slices turkey bacon
- 12 oz. egg noodles
- 1 1/2 C. cheddar cheese, shredded
- 1 1/2 C. sour cream
- 1 onion, chopped
- 2 tbsp butter

Directions

1. Set your oven to 375 degrees F before doing anything else.
2. Heat a skillet oven on medium-high heat and cook half of the bacon till browned completely.
3. Transfer the bacon onto a paper towel lined plate to drain and then crumble it.
4. Prepare the egg noodles according to the package's directions.
5. Drain well and transfer into a bowl with 2 tbsp of the butter and toss to coat.
6. In a large casserole dish, place the ingredients in the layers of 1/4 of the noodles, followed by 1/4 of the sour cream, 1/4 of the cheddar cheese, 1/4 of the bacon and 1/4 of the onion.
7. Repeat the layers three times more.
8. Cook everything in the oven for about 30 minutes.

MUSHROOM
Casserole

🍲 Prep Time: 20 mins
🕐 Total Time: 45 mins

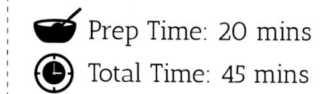

Servings per Recipe: 6
Calories   275.5
Fat   10.2g
Cholesterol   86.4mg
Sodium   219.3mg
Carbohydrates   35.3g
Protein   11.2g

Ingredients

1/2 lb wide egg noodles
Butter, for sautéing
1/2 lb mushroom, sliced
1 large onion, sliced
3 oz. cheese, grated
1 egg, beaten
1/4 C. breadcrumbs
salt and pepper
1 oz. cold butter

Directions

1. Set your oven to 325 degrees F before doing anything else and grease a casserole dish.
2. In a large pan of lightly salted boiling water, cook the egg noodles for about 7 minutes.
3. Drain well and transfer into the prepared casserole dish.
4. Meanwhile in a large skillet, melt the butter and sauté the onion and mushrooms till tender.
5. With a slotted spoon, transfer the mushrooms mixture in the casserole dish, leaving the butter in the skillet.
6. Place most of the cheese over the mushroom mixture and mix well. (Reserve some cheese for topping.)
7. In the same skillet, add the beaten egg and little boiling water and stir to combine with the remaining butter.
8. Stir till a sauce forms.
9. Place the sauce over the noodle mixture evenly, followed by the remaining cheese and breadcrumbs.
10. Place the cold butter over the casserole in the shape of dots evenly and cook everything in the oven for about 20 - 25 minutes.

Weeknight Dinner
Noodles

Prep Time: 10 mins
Total Time: 20 mins

Servings per Recipe: 6
Calories   571.0
Fat   18.8g
Cholesterol   195.3mg
Sodium   1048.8mg
Carbohydrates   66.8g
Protein   30.9g

Ingredients

- 16 oz. egg noodles
- 2 tbsp vegetable oil
- 1 tbsp butter
- 10 cloves garlic, minced
- 1 scallion, chopped
- 1 lb shrimp, shells removed and de-veined
- 1 1/2 C. whole milk
- 1 C. grated parmesan cheese
- 2 tbsp butter
- 1/8-1/4 tsp cayenne pepper
- 1 tbsp lime juice

Directions

1. Prepare the egg noodles according to the package's directions, and drain well.
2. Meanwhile in a large skillet, melt the butter and oil and sauté the scallion and garlic for about 2 minutes.
3. Add the Shrimp and stir fry them for about 2 minutes.
4. Stir in the remaining ingredients and cook, stirring continuously for about 5 minutes.
5. Add the noodles and toss to coat
6. Serve immediately.

TARRAGON AND SAGE
Egg Noodles

Prep Time: 10 mins
Total Time: 25 mins

Servings per Recipe: 4
Calories 316.3
Fat 11.3g
Cholesterol 70.7mg
Sodium 395.5mg
Carbohydrates 45.3g
Protein 8.8g

Ingredients

8 oz. egg noodles
3 - 4 tbsp butter
1 1/2 C. shredded carrots
1/3 C. chopped fresh parsley
1 tsp dried rubbed sage
1/2 tsp tarragon
1/2 tsp garlic powder
1/2 tsp salt
1/2 tsp pepper

Directions

1. Prepare the egg noodles according to the package's directions, and drain well.
2. In the same pan, melt the butter and cook the carrots, covered for about 6 - 8 minutes, stirring occasionally.
3. Stir in the remaining ingredients.
4. Add the noodles and toss to coat well.

Perfect Buttered Noodles

Prep Time: 5 mins
Total Time: 20 mins

Servings per Recipe: 6
Calories   448.3
Fat   19.9g
Cholesterol   108.1mg
Sodium   311.9mg
Carbohydrates   55.0g
Protein   12.6g

Ingredients

16 oz. egg noodles
1/2 C. butter
1/4 C. chopped onion
6 fresh sage leaves, chopped
1/4 tsp salt
1/4 tsp black pepper
1/4-1/2 C. fresh grated parmesan cheese

Directions

1. Prepare the egg noodles according to the package's directions.
2. In a skillet, melt the butter and sauté the sage and onion for about 5 minutes.
3. Add the noodles, salt and black pepper and toss to coat.
4. Sprinkle with the cheese and serve.

AMERICAN/FRENCH
Noodle Soup

Prep Time: 30 mins
Total Time: 1 hr 15 mins

Servings per Recipe: 12
Calories 403.6
Fat 17.7g
Cholesterol 104.8mg
Sodium 873.7mg
Carbohydrates 29.3g
Protein 30.3g

Ingredients

3 lb. bone-in chicken breasts
1 stalk celery, leaves attached, cut in chunks
1 carrot, cut in chunks
1 onion, quartered
1 tbsp seasoning salt
10 -12 whole black peppercorns
4 quarts water
2 chicken bouillon cubes
4 cans cream of chicken soup, reduced fat preferred
1 (12 oz.) packages wide egg noodles
1 tbsp minced onion
dried parsley, to taste
additional seasoning salt, to taste
black pepper, to taste
red pepper flakes, just a pinch

Directions

1. In a large Dutch oven, mix together the chicken, carrot, celery, onion, 1 tbsp seasoning salt, peppercorns and water and simmer till chicken is fully cooked.
2. Transfer the chicken into a bowl and remove the bones and skin, then shred it.
3. Strain the broth completely.
4. Return the broth to the pan and bring everything to a boil.
5. Stir in the noodles and cook them for about 6 minutes.
6. Reduce the heat and stir in the bouillon cubes.
7. Add the chicken soup and gently, stir to combine.
8. Stir in the cooked chicken and remaining ingredients and serve hot.

Simply Delicious Noodles

Prep Time: 5 mins
Total Time: 25 mins

Servings per Recipe: 5
Calories   218.9
Fat   8.8g
Cholesterol   43.8mg
Sodium   126.5mg
Carbohydrates   27.0g
Protein   8.5g

Ingredients

3 C. uncooked medium egg noodles
2 C. broccoli florets
1 (10 oz.) cans cream of chicken and broccoli soup
1/2 C. sour cream
1/3 C. grated parmesan cheese
1/8 tsp pepper
1/4 tsp garlic powder

Directions

1. In large pan prepare the noodles according to the package's directions.
2. In the last 5 minutes cooking, add the broccoli and then drain.
3. In the same pan, add the noodle mixture and remaining ingredients on medium heat and cook, stirring occasionally till everything is heated completely.

SHIBUYA CROSSING
Egg Noodles

Prep Time: 10 mins
Total Time: 10 mins

Servings per Recipe: 6
Calories   181.6
Fat   4.2g
Cholesterol   31.9mg
Sodium   381.4mg
Carbohydrates   29.3g
Protein   6.3g

Ingredients

1/2 lb egg noodles, cooked
1 tbsp sesame oil
1 carrot, julienned
1 green onion, chopped
1 tsp sesame seeds
Sauce
1 garlic clove, minced
2 tbsp white vinegar
2 tbsp soy sauce
1 tsp ginger, ground
1 tbsp wasabi paste

Directions

1. In a bowl, mix together cooked noodles and sesame oil and refrigerate to chill.
2. In another bowl, mix together all the sauce ingredients and refrigerate to chill.
3. Just before serving, in the bowl of noodles, add the sauce, green onion and carrot and mix well.
4. Serve with a topping of sesame seeds.

Classic Yankee Noodles

Prep Time: 15 mins
Total Time: 27 mins

Servings per Recipe: 4
Calories	355.4
Fat	18.3g
Cholesterol	88.9mg
Sodium	853.4mg
Carbohydrates	19.1g
Protein	27.6g

Ingredients

- 1/4 lb mushroom, chopped roughly
- 2 stalks celery, chopped roughly
- 1 medium onion, chopped roughly
- 2 garlic cloves, chopped roughly
- 1 lb lean ground beef
- 2/3 C. fine plain breadcrumbs
- 1/2 tsp salt
- 1/4 tsp pepper
- 2 tbsp butter
- 1 C. beef broth
- 2 tbsp tomato paste
- hot cooked egg noodles with butter

Directions

1. Set the oven to broiler and arrange the oven rack about 4-inches from heating element.
2. Line a broiler pan with some foil sheets.
3. In a bowl, mix together the beef, 1/3 C. of the breadcrumbs, salt, black pepper and half of the all vegetables.
4. Make about 1/2-inch thick patties from the mixture.
5. Arrange the patties onto prepared broiler pan and cook under the broiler for about 5 minutes.
6. Flip the patties and cook under the broiler for about 7 minutes.
7. Meanwhile in a large skillet, melt the butter and on medium-high heat, sauté the remaining vegetables for about 2 minutes.
8. Add the remaining breadcrumbs, tomato paste and broth and bring to a boil.
9. Reduce the heat to medium-low and simmer, covered for about 5 minutes.
10. Place the vegetable mixture over the patties and serve alongside the noodles.

Manufactured by Amazon.ca
Acheson, AB